Little-Known
FACTS
ABOUT
Well-Known
PLACES

WALT DISNEY WORLD

{ Little-Known
FACTS
ABOUT
Well-Known
PLACES }

WALT DISNEY WORLD

Laurie Flannery

FALL RIVER PRESS

New York

FALL RIVER PRESS

New York

An Imprint of Sterling Publishing
387 Park Avenue South
New York, NY 10016

ISBN 978-1-4351-3323-5

Distributed in Canada by Sterling Publishing
c/o Canadian Manda Group, 165 Dufferin Street
Toronto, Ontario, Canada M6K 3H6
Distributed in the United Kingdom by GMC Distribution Services
Castle Place, 166 High Street, Lewes, East Sussex, England BN7 1XU
Distributed in Australia by Capricorn Link (Australia) Pty. Ltd.
P.O. Box 704, Windsor, NSW 2756, Australia

For information about custom editions, special sales, and premium and
corporate purchases, please contact Sterling Special Sales at 800-805-5489
or specialsales@sterlingpublishing.com.

Manufactured in China

4 6 8 10 9 7 5 3

www.sterlingpublishing.com

INTRODUCTION

It's the most visited vacation spot in the entire world. Its icon, Cinderella Castle, is the most photographed building on the planet. It's the place where dreams come true and magic seems to be around every corner.

Walt Disney World was the dream of a man whose imagination knew no limits. It was designed and built not just by "engineers," but by what the Walt Disney Company calls "Imagineers"—special individuals who combine technical skills with creative thoughts that are sprinkled with fairy dust.

Everyone who works inside the park is referred to as a "cast member," since every sight, smell, sound, and feeling is part of the "show." The Walt Disney Company weaves incredible detail into everything it creates:

hidden tributes to important people in Walt Disney World's history, stories told through every attraction, and even a special meaning in the nightly fireworks displays!

Spanning 25,000 acres, a quarter of which is dedicated to land preservation, this massive resort is truly one of a kind. Walt Disney World specializes in "How'd they do that?!"—making the impossible seem very, very possible.

It's a place like no other. From its four theme parks—Magic Kingdom, Epcot, Animal Kingdom, and Hollywood Studios—to its multiple resorts, restaurants, water-recreation facilities, golf courses, and even race-car driving track, this entertainment extravaganza has something for everyone.

This small volume of trivia lets you in on some of Walt Disney World's secrets, history, and neat little stories. Ready to pull back the curtain and take a peek behind the magic of Walt Disney World? Read on...

Look for these other
titles in the series:

Little-Known
FACTS
ABOUT
Well-Known
PLACES

DISNEYLAND ✦ IRELAND
ITALY ✦ NEW ORLEANS
NEW YORK ✦ PARIS ✦ TEXAS

Walt Disney World covers nearly 39 square miles, or about 25,000 acres—a footprint that's almost as big as San Francisco or Boston. Of that area, less than 35 percent has been developed. One quarter of the land is permanently designated as a wilderness preserve.

All decked out: Mickey Mouse has more than 290 outfits in his wardrobe, including a tuxedo, football uniform, sorcerer outfit, and scuba wetsuit. Minnie Mouse's closet holds more than 200 outfits, including evening dresses and a cheerleader uniform.

How many stone blocks were used to create Cinderella Castle, the most photographed building in the world? None. The building's shell is actually a steel skeleton covered in fiberglass. The castle was built to withstand hurricane-force winds exceeding 90mph.

The Circle-Vision 360 movie seen in Epcot's China pavilion was filmed by a dedicated crew that carried a 300-pound camera up 4,500 steps of the Huangshan Mountain in Anhui Province.

Epcot's Land pavilion has a one-of-a-kind tomato "tree" growing in its experimental greenhouses. The plant yields thousands of golf-ball-size tomatoes from a single vine.

The plant's predecessor produced a world-record-breaking 32,194 tomatoes. The Land pavilion also is home to a cucumber "tree," whose predecessor produced 2,563 vegetables in one year.

Walt Disney World employs more than 62,000 people, including at least 58,000 cast members. That's more than twice the number of employees at the Pentagon (23,000), one of the world's largest office complexes. WDW is, in fact, the largest single-site employer in the United States.

team of Imagineers is the creative force behind all the Disney magic. Walt Disney Imagineering (WDI) is responsible for design and development throughout the Walt Disney Company. The department was founded in 1952 under the original name WED (Walter Elias Disney) Enterprises.

Taking care of the furry contingents of Animal Kingdom is no small job. Each year the Animal Programs Team performs more than 600 wellness check-ups on the Kingdom's elephants, giraffes, and other residents. Among their fascinating triumphs: They've placed an artificial eye in a fish, and have even performed surgery on a tarantula! They've analyzed 40,000 scat samples—no wonder, since the menu includes more than 2,000 pounds of vegetation daily and 80,000 crickets per month!

Expedition Everest covers approximately six acres and reaches almost 200 feet high, the tallest of the 18 theme-park mountain attractions that Disney's Imagineering team has created worldwide. Inside, it's a technological superstructure with three distinct features: the detailed rock-work face of the mountain, the high-speed roller-coaster ride, and an audio-animatronic Yeti.

The Walt Disney World Development Team has always appreciated fine craftsmanship. It often seeks unique antiques for use within the complex, such as Prince Charming Regal Carrousel (formerly Cinderella's Golden Carrousel). Originally crafted in 1917 and dubbed the Liberty Carousel, it once entertained children and adults at the Palace Garden Amusement Park in Detroit, Michigan. In 1928 it was moved to Maplewood Olympic Park in Maplewood, New Jersey, where it held court until Disney purchased it in 1967. The Disney team then completely refurbished the ride, hand-painting each horse with meticulous detail. Of the 90 horses, 72 still date back to the original craftsmen. Even Cinderella has her own horse on the ride—look for the gold ribbon on its tail. The circular wonder is the oldest attraction in the Magic Kingdom.

Walt Disney World was not the original name of the resort. It was simply going to be called "Disney World." After Walt's death in 1966, his brother Roy O. Disney postponed his retirement to take control of the project. As the resort neared completion, Roy changed its name to "Walt Disney World," explaining, "People will always know this was Walt's dream."

Do you know why the window shutters on the buildings in Liberty Square are positioned at an angle? In colonial times, the upper hinges of windows were usually made of leather straps, causing shutters to hang loosely. This helped conserve metal, an important commodity at the time. The Liberty Square shutter hinges are all constructed of metal, but were intentionally slanted for a more authentic look.

Epcot's famous, globe-shaped Spaceship Earth actually was named by Buckminster Fuller, who also developed the geodesic sphere's architectural form. Spaceship Earth was the first of its kind to be constructed. Since then the geodesic sphere has been reproduced more than 300,000 times worldwide.

For many years Disney has offered collectible pins in its parks, but the tradition of pin trading wasn't introduced until the Millennium Celebration launched in October 1999. It's become so popular over the years that it's now a staple at Walt Disney World, Disneyland, Disneyland Paris, and on Disney Cruise Line ships. Traders can swap with cast members sporting pins on a special lanyard or even other pin-wearing travelers. Traders also gather at dozens of official pin-trading stations around WDW. Disney releases thousands of new pins each year and holds events for the Pin Trading Society.

isney's Pop Century Resort's monstrous eight-track tapes are more than 35 feet tall, exactly 80 times the size of a real one. The "tape" of the eight-track is one foot wide—or 48 times the size of the real quarter-inch tape.

The bats living within the Maharajah Jungle Trek at Animal Kingdom have been trained by the Disney team to do something bat experts claimed could never be accomplished— respond to an audio cue. When a dog whistle is blown, the bats head inside for dinner—fruit is on the menu, by the way!

When executives decided to build WDW in Florida, the company devised an approach to purchase the 47-square-mile area of land from multiple owners through shell companies. Walt feared that once people knew he was buying the land, values would skyrocket. You may notice some of those shell company names—Tomahawk Properties, Bay Lake Properties, Compass East Corporation, and Latin American Development— are displayed in the windows above the Market House on Main Street U.S.A.

On November 17, 1973, the Contemporary Resort was host to President Richard Nixon's famous "I Am Not a Crook" hourlong televised speech, given in front of 400 Associated Press managing editors (who were gathered for their annual meeting). The speech signaled the beginning of the end of the Nixon presidency and announced a new era in American politics.

Where can you find one of the most advanced multisensory attractions in the world? Check out The Twilight Zone Tower of Terror at Disney's Hollywood Studios. You'll experience visual, audio, and olfactory special effects in random ride-and-drop sequences that make each trip a unique experience. The Tower of Terror is also the first attraction in the world that actually determines its own ride sequence.

What WDW park icon took a crew of thousands more than 18 months to complete? The 14-story-tall Tree of Life in Animal Kingdom. The manmade tree is 145 feet high and stretches 170 feet across at the root base. A team of 20 artists carved 325 beautiful animal figures in the tree trunk. That's not all. The multicolored leaves adorning the tree—103,000 in all—were attached by hand.

Keep an eye out for the many "Hidden Mickeys" that can be found all around the resort. Originally, Hidden Mickeys were two smaller circles on top of one large circle incorporated into a design, creating the familiar head of Mickey Mouse. Today, people spot Hidden Mickeys in many different forms. Some of the other styles include a distorted three circle version of Mickey's head, or even the image of his whole body. Imagineers take great joy in using Hidden Mickeys in both obvious and subtle ways. An example can be found in the Zip-A-Dee-Doo-Dah scene of Splash Mountain: Mickey is to the right of the riverboat, lying on his back in the pink clouds.

Walt Disney World College Program has been around for more than 30 years, recruiting students from all over the world to come work in the parks and earn up to nine college credits. The company provides housing (for a fee), bus transportation to and from work, and social events (pool parties, networking events, etc.). WDW offers classes for which students can get credit at their home colleges. There's a guest speaker series, too. After completing the college program, students can then apply for a professional internship with Disney.

If you've ever visited the African savanna, you may know that acacia trees are the mainstay of the landscape. Animal Kingdom's Kilimanjaro Safaris, however, is pulling a switch-a-roo on its residents by carefully trimming Florida's native southern live oak trees to mimic the flat-topped acacias. Disney claims the giraffes don't mind munching on these substitutes.

Mickey's PhilharMagic 3-D film spectacular, in the Magic Kingdom's Fantasyland Concert Hall, features one of the largest seamless projection screens in the world. It's 150 feet wide and 28 feet high, providing the most immersive wraparound display Disney has ever created.

Wishes, a 12-minute fireworks program staged above the Magic Kingdom each night and narrated by Jiminy Cricket, is the biggest display ever produced for the park. It contains 683 individual pieces of pyrotechnics. Some of the special effects were developed specifically for the show, which also incorporates Tinker Bell's famous flight from the top of Cinderella Castle.

The Hall of Presidents, one of WDW's original attractions, features every president who has served our country, including current president Barack Obama. But why, then, are only 43 heads of state on stage if Obama is our 44th president? President Grover Cleveland served two non-consecutive terms, making him our 22nd and 24th president.

WOW estimates that of the multitudes of Floridians who applied for a job at the resort before it opened, only about one in every 12 applicants was actually hired. In early 1972, just a few months after opening day, the park employed approximately 8,000 people. Disney estimates that about 96,000 people applied for cast member positions in those early days. That's 1½ times the number of spectators Heinz Field can accommodate for a Pittsburgh Steelers game.

"Cast members"—the term Disney uses to refer to employees who work in its theme parks—include individuals who dress up as characters, hotel staff, restaurant workers, and ride operators. At WDW, everything is considered part of the "show," and Disney employees are all part of the show's "cast."

After Walt's death, Navy Admiral Joe Fowler and Army General Joe Potter were enlisted to oversee construction of the Magic Kingdom. Admiral Fowler had previously handled the construction of Disneyland in California, and General Potter had managed both the building of the Panama Canal and the 1964 World's Fair complex, making these men qualified to take on the biggest private construction project in the country at the time.

The Rock N' Roller Coaster Starring Aerosmith attraction at Disney's Hollywood Studios lays claim to several design firsts. It's the first launching roller coaster, utilizing linear synchronous motor technology (catapulting you from zero to 60mph in less than three seconds); the first to have inversions (three, to be exact); and the first coaster to be synchronized to music.

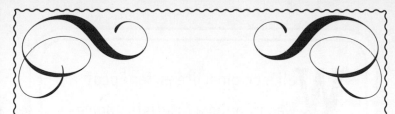

In the Himalayan region, wood is so scarce that buildings typically are made of compressed earth block and stacked stone, and then decorated with wood carvings. Disney wanted to recreate that authenticity in the village buildings of Serka Zong, which is part of the Expedition Everest: Legend of the Forbidden Mountain attraction in Animal Kingdom. The company commissioned Nepalese and Balinese craftsmen to create more than 1,000 Sal wood and teak carvings that now adorn this exhibit.

Walt's original dream for Epcot was to build a futuristic, dome-enclosed city for 20,000 residents. He wanted his community to showcase the "ingenuity and imagination of American free enterprise." Here, problems of urban living could be studied and addressed. The city would be designed as a hub and spoke system, with industry at the center and residential and recreational areas on the outskirts. Cars and trucks would operate underground only and the "pedestrian would be king." Sadly, the project was too ambitious—even for Walt Disney.

The Many Adventures of Winnie the Pooh opened in 1999, replacing the Magic Kingdom's popular original attraction, Mr. Toad's Wild Ride. You still can find Mr. Toad if you look hard enough, though. Observant visitors inside the Winnie the Pooh ride may spot a picture of Mr. Toad handing the deed of the ride to Owl. You also can catch a glimpse of his statue at the Pet Cemetery at the Haunted Mansion.

One of the hottest dining spots in the Magic Kingdom, Cinderella's Royal Table, originally was named King Stefan's Banquet Hall. King Stefan was a misleading moniker, since he was dad to a different princess: Sleeping Beauty. The name change went into effect in 1997.

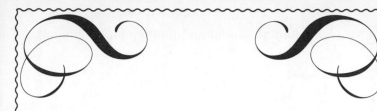

Nearly all the animals that inhabit WDW's Animal Kingdom first lived at other zoos or conservation facilities. Many animals had to make "pitstops" between their old home and Animal Kingdom due to quarantine rules, acclimation, and park construction delays. The bat population now living in Maharajah Jungle Trek, for example, hung out for several months at one of the world's preeminent conservancies, the Lubee Foundation in Gainesville, Florida.

Disney employs more than 600 horticulture professionals who plant more than 3 million annuals on the property each year and care for 4,000 acres of gardens and landscapes. That's nearly five times the size of New York City's Central Park! These experts perform many tasks to keep the resort beautiful in addition to providing the proper physical environment for the residents of the Animal Kingdom.

The Mr. Potato Head audio-animatronic figure at the Toy Story Mania! attraction at Hollywood Studios claims several firsts at WDW. Compared to any other audio-animatronic figure created by Walt Disney Imagineering...

- Imagineers spent the most time programming Mr. Potato Head.

- He's capable of speaking more lines of dialogue than any other audio-animatronic.

- He's the first whose mouth appears to form words and vowel sounds.

- He has animated eyes that look directly at guests when speaking to them.

hrough Disney's Harvest Program, founded in 1998, the resort's excess prepared but unserved food is collected and distributed to state agencies by the Disney Harvest truck in cooperation with the Second Harvest Food Bank of Central Florida. WDW donates nearly 50,000 pounds of food per month.

isney's effort to be "green" includes the production of more than 30 tons of fruit and vegetables per year, which are grown at the Land pavilion at Epcot. The area features farming concepts and technologies that encourage sustainable agriculture. This includes specialized irrigation systems that reduce waste and boost crop production in ways that are "greener" and kinder to the environment. The produce is then served at WDW restaurants.

The Magic Kingdom's 189-foot-high Cinderella Castle held the title for the tallest structure at the resort, until it lost its seat to the 199-foot-tall Twilight Zone Tower of Terror at Disney's Hollywood Studios. But even the Tower of Terror couldn't hold onto the title once Expedition Everest—reaching just shy of 200 feet—was constructed at Animal Kingdom.

78 million
Coca-Cola products consumed
on the property annually

10 million
hamburgers devoured by
guests each year

5.3 million
bags of popcorn enjoyed by
visitors annually

When WDW opened its resort for the first time it was to a crowd of 10,000 on October 1, 1971. The lucky Windsors—Bill Jr., Marty, Jay, and Lee—were the very first family to walk through the entrance gates. They went home with wonderful memories, as well as lifetime passes. Three college students were actually first in line, but they were passed over by Disney officials for the more wholesome-looking Windsor family. On October 22, 1979, eight-year-old Kurt Miller from Kingsville, Maryland, became the 100-millionth visitor at the Magic Kingdom. WDW estimates that 40 million people visit the property each year.

Epcot's Earth Globe, the centerpiece of IllumiNations: Reflections of Earth fireworks/laser show, contains more than 180,000 light emitting diodes (LEDs) that illuminate the continents on the globe each night. It's the world's first spherical video display system, employing 15,500 miniature video screens, and it has been called one of Imagineering's most complicated pieces of show equipment. The barge that carries Earth Globe and some of the arsenal of the IllumiNations fireworks is floated out into the lagoon each day. The globe weighs a hefty 350,000 pounds.

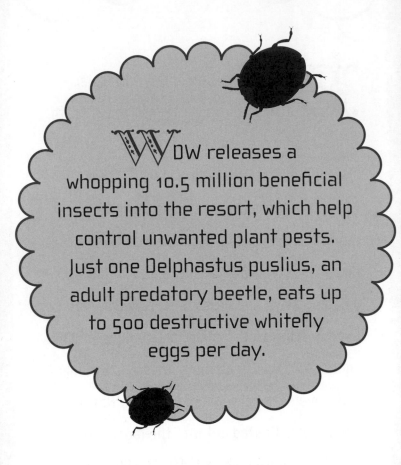

WDW releases a whopping 10.5 million beneficial insects into the resort, which help control unwanted plant pests. Just one Delphastus puslius, an adult predatory beetle, eats up to 500 destructive whitefly eggs per day.

An enormous Big Wheel toy is the architectural centerpiece of the courtyard at Disney's Pop Century Resort (1970s section). The official-looking weight-limit sticker on the sculpture states that it can accommodate a child rider up to 877 pounds!

Approximately 1,000 animals live in Animal Kingdom, and more than 150 species have reproduced in the park since it opened. The very first birth was a kudu, which is a large, African antelope. Disney has also had 17 Micronesian Kingfisher chicks hatch on the premises, raising the world population of these very rare feathered friends by 20 percent!

If you were a 350-foot-tall Mickey, where would you find the perfect sorcerer's hat? Try Disney's Hollywood Studios' park icon. At 122 feet tall and weighing in at 156 tons, this giant-size hat centerpiece was installed for 2001's 100 Years of Magic celebration. Its "official" hat size is 606⅞!

One of the world's largest surfing lagoons, Typhoon Lagoon, located near Old Key West Resort, measures approximately 109,000 square feet and contains almost 3 million gallons of water. It offers three whitewater rafting adventures, three water slides where guests can clock in at 30mph, and even a unique, 362,000-gallon coral-reef environment for divers.

Did you know the Magic Kingdom is actually built on the "second floor" of the park? Most visitors never see or even hear about the ground level, called the "utilidor," short for "utility corridor." Because Central Florida's water table is just two feet below ground level, this specialized series of corridors and service facilities was constructed on ground level. It was covered with excess silt and debris Disney excavated from Bay Lake. Then the Magic Kingdom park was built on top. The utilidor nerve center consists of more than a mile of corridors and areas like storage rooms, wardrobe, offices, a cafeteria, a trash removal system, and all support services for cast members.

Disney uses a well-known film technique called forced perspective to create a larger-than-life feeling in many areas of the resort, especially the Magic Kingdom. Cinderella Castle is a prime example. Although it's only 189 feet high, it seems much taller. How? One example: Disney shrinks the size of the stones and windows as they get higher, creating the illusion of height.

When WDW opened in 1971, admission to the park was $3.50 for adults, $2.50 for kids 12–17, and $1 for those ages 3–11. Ride tickets labeled A through E (E being the "best" rides such as 20,000 Leagues Under the Sea), cost extra. Other rides and attractions, such as the Diamond Horseshoe Revue, were free. In preparation of Epcot's opening in the early 1980s, these A–E tickets were phased out in favor of simpler, all-in-one general admission prices.

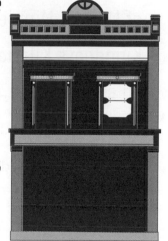

What's nearly the same size as the entire Magic Kingdom but gives you a chance to meet lions, giraffes, and zebras (oh my!) instead of Mickey, Minnie, and Goofy? Animal Kingdom's Kilimanjaro Safaris, spanning an approximate 110 acres. It's the largest attraction in WDW or in any Disney theme park worldwide.

What a wardrobe! Boasting more than 2.5 million individual costume pieces and nearly eight miles of costume racks, the largest working wardrobe in the world belongs to WDW. The Disney Creative Costuming team uses more than 650,000 yards of fabric each year, which—stretched end to end—would cover the 369-mile distance between New York City and Pittsburgh, Pennsylvania!

Ol' Man Island recreation area at Disney's Port Orleans Resort celebrated Earth Day in 1991 by receiving its centerpiece: a towering, 55-foot-tall tree. The Disney team moved the southern live oak, weighing nearly 85 tons, 12 miles across the resort to reside in its new home.

Ever wanted to see the parks in style and even avoid some of the waiting? Try booking an individual VIP Tour, a service offered at WDW since it opened. Experienced cast members will tailor a tour to suit your party's needs, including arranging priority seating for all resort restaurants, special viewing areas for all parades and live stage shows, and even shopping for you if you desire. They can't help you skip lines for the rides entirely but can arrange more immediate access for FastPass attractions. (FastPass allows visitors to obtain a ticket that gives a one-hour window to return and access the ride with little or no wait time.)

If you want to rub elbows with Mickey Mouse while dining at the resort, you can catch the Big Cheese at only three locations: Ohana's breakfast service at Disney's Polynesian Resort, the Land pavilion's Garden Grill restaurant for dinner, and the Contemporary Resort's Chef Mickey's Fun Time Buffet for breakfast and dinner.

What percentage of recycled concrete and metals were used to construct the Treehouse Villas at WDW's Saratoga Springs Resort? More than 65 percent, which translates to a whopping 5,178 tons of building materials.

If you stand directly in front of the Cinderella Fountain statue (near Tinker Bell's Treasures shop in Fantasyland) and look at just the right angle, you'll notice the painting of the crown in the background ornamentation appears to sit perfectly on this beloved princess' head.

Beating the heat: The lions in Kilimanjaro Safaris originally were from an Oregon zoo and had a hard time adjusting to Florida's heat. They  often would retreat from visitors' view to a shaded area. So Imagineers installed an air-conditioning system around the lions' promontory. Now folks have a better chance of seeing the kings of the savannah.

A note written on Hollywood Studios' Tower of Terror stationery in the attraction's library states: "Porcelains of Europe, although susceptible to earthquake damage, are an important element in films and attractions of Hollywood." If you are familiar with WDW, you can guess that this is no random message. It actually refers to a real collection of porcelain that was slated to be used for props in Tower of Terror. However, just before they were shipped from storage in California, much of the collection was damaged when the Northbridge Earthquake hit.

Fans get a thrill seeing Indie run from that famous boulder in the Hollywood Studios' live show, Indiana Jones Epic Stunt Spectacular. Disney's 12-foot-diameter "boulder" weighs 440 pounds and is made of rubber. (So it'd still hurt if it ran over you!)

What contains more than 2,385 billion gallons of water and covers 596 acres? The two biggest lakes at WDW: Bay Lake and the adjoining Seven Seas Lagoon. Disney's Seven Seas Lagoon is manmade, but Bay Lake is a natural body of water.

Before Test Track—a high-speed vehicle simulation ride—opened in Epcot in 1999, the fastest "ride" at WDW actually was a bus! Park buses are allowed to speed up to 50mph, according to local speed limits. The cars of Test Track blow the buses away at 65mph.

What annual festival takes more than a year to prepare, requires approximately 24,000 work hours by 600 horticulturists, and features 11 musical acts for its signature concert? The Annual Epcot International Flower and Garden Festival, which runs for 75 days each year. Visit during this time period in the spring, and you'll see 600 butterflies at Fawn's Butterfly House and more than 30 million flowers throughout Epcot alone.

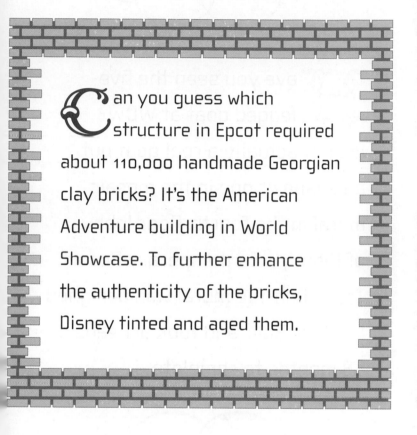

Can you guess which structure in Epcot required about 110,000 handmade Georgian clay bricks? It's the American Adventure building in World Showcase. To further enhance the authenticity of the bricks, Disney tinted and aged them.

Have you seen the five-legged goat at WDW? It's not actually a real goat but an image of one in the mosaic mural in the fourth-floor lobby of Disney's Contemporary Resort. This 1,800-tile mural was designed by Mary Blair and took artisans 18 months to complete.

If you read music, perhaps you can guess what melody the notes on the registration desk at Disney's Port Orleans Resort–French Quarter represent. It's the first verse of "When the Saints Go Marching In."

Which one of the tallest mountain attractions at WDW opened in 1980? Big Thunder Mountain in Magic Kingdom's Frontierland. It took 15 years to plan, tons of steel and concrete, hundreds of rock makers, 4,000 gallons of paint, and 900,000 gallons of water to create realistic, red-rock buttes and mine buildings inspired by Arizona's Monument Valley.

Most people go to WDW for thrills and chills, but did you know the property also has three spas? The Mandara Spa at the Dolphin Resort, the Spa at Saratoga Springs, and the high-end Grand Floridian Spa and Health Club. The extensive services include several kinds of massages, such as Mandara Hot Stone Therapy, and treatments like Elemis Exotic Coconut Rub and Milk Ritual Wrap, as well as the Maple Sugar Body Polish. Ahh...

When you compare Cinderella Castle to Neuschwanstein Castle in Bavaria, it seems fairly obvious that it was Disney's main inspiration. But Imagineers drew their design ideas from several other castles, as well: the castle in the film *Cinderella*; the real-life Palace of Versailles; Fontainebleau; and the chateaus of Chambord, Chaumont, and Chenonceau—all in France.

Love roses? Almost 13,000 of them can be found at WDW throughout the year. Removing the blooms past their prime is one big job, though. It takes more than 4,000 hours of work per year, about the equivalent of two full-time horticulturists.

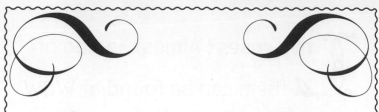

Animal Kingdom's Dinosaur attraction's "Time Rover" transportation devices may be the most complicated in the amusement park industry. Disney wanted riders to feel as though they're driving through ruts and over stones and tree trunks. Instead of creating a bumpy track, the Time Rovers themselves were made to simulate the experience. Programmers can recode the software to adjust the experience.

What WDW building has a sign over its entrance stating "Home of Excellence"? That would be Central Shops, a facility most visitors never enter, unless they take the Backstage Magic tour. This is where Disney "magic" is built, refurbished, and repaired, including the fabrication of buildings, props, and even rides.

Did you know some well-known "celebrities" at WDW actually wear wigs made of human hair? It's not who you think, though. Disney's live performing cast members wear synthetic hair wigs—but many audio-animatronic figures, like members of the Hall of Presidents, wear human-hair wigs.

Did you know that Mickey Mouse and Donald Duck are cleverly hidden in the Indiana Jones section of the Great Movie Ride in Disney's Hollywood Studios? Watch for the "Hidden Mickey" hieroglyphic in the first section of the ride, on the left side of your car just past a large white pillar. (It's so popular WDW even made a commemorative pin of this Hidden Mickey.) If you look closely at the Egyptian wall tiles, you also may find Star Wars' R2-D2 and C-3PO.

The majority of Donald Duck's voice in Mickey's PhilharMagic attraction was created from older recordings of classic performances by Clarence "Ducky" Nash, the original voice of Donald. The current voice of Donald, Tony Anselmo, added the lines that had not previously been recorded by Ducky.

Who was Minnie Moo? As you can guess, she was a (real) cow. The interesting part of this story is the mark—what appears to be a silhouette of Mickey's ears—she was born with on her side. Destined for WDW, she arrived in 1990 and grazed at Grandma Duck's Farm, which was in Mickey's Birthdayland, until she was moved to the Petting Farm at Fort Wilderness Resort in 1996. She passed away in 2001.

WALT DISNEY WORLD
FACTS

There are two Foo Dogs (Chinese lion statues) standing guard at the entrance of the Yong Feng Shangdian Department Store in Epcot's China pavilion. If the lion's foot is resting on the globe, it means that it's a male. The one with a foot on its cub signifies it's a female.

Victoria & Albert's at Disney's Grand Floridian Resort is the only AAA five-diamond restaurant in Central Florida and has been recognized with an Award of Excellence by *Wine Spectator* as well. With only 18 tables in the main dining room and another five in the private "fireplace room," dining here is an upscale experience. Foodies take note: You'll want to reserve the most exclusive table at the resort, the Chef's Table, in the very heart of the kitchen. You can watch the entire meal being prepared by a top-notch team. Here, you'll be served up to 13 specially prepared courses, which are personally explained by Chef Scott Hunne.

Although Disney's attention to detail is legendary, Walt asked Imagineers to design the storefront windows on Main Street U.S.A. in the Magic Kingdom closer to the ground than they would have been in their time period of the early 1900s. He felt it was more important for children to be able to see inside.

The Magic Kingdom's Crystal Palace, which serves as the transition from Main Street U.S.A. to Adventureland, was inspired by several pieces of architecture, including the Royal Botanic Gardens at Kew in England, New York's Crystal Palace, and the San Francisco Conservatory of Flowers.

When Epcot opened in 1982, Walt's wife Lillian presided over the dedication ceremony of the World Fellowship Fountain, which features dancing water set to music. At the dedication ceremony, representatives from 23 countries attended to "feed" the fountain with water from their own lakes and rivers. Disney wanted the fountain to represent the commonalities and shared aspirations of people around the world.

Why did the creation of the Hollywood Studios park mark a new era for the Imagineering staff? This was essentially the first Disney theme park to be designed and developed without significant input from the first generation of legendary Imagineers. This "new" crew of Imagineers worked with their predecessors on the design of Epcot, Tokyo Disneyland, and many other large-scale projects. But the generational transfer of knowledge, tradition, and storytelling was finally put to the test with this park's installation.

Dying to surf the perfect wave at Typhoon Lagoon's wave pool? Surfing is prohibited during park hours, but you can surf after hours or before the park opens in the morning. WDW books Private Surf Parties for up to 25 wave riders so they can enjoy the 2.75-million-gallon wave pool all by themselves. Waves up to six feet tall will roll out every 90 seconds, giving you 100 chances for a great ride in just three hours.

Walt originally intended to build two additions to Main Street in Disneyland, California, sprouting off of Center Street. The first, called Edison Square, was to celebrate American innovation, and the second was Liberty Square, a tribute to colonial America. However, the upcoming American bicentennial celebration was only five years away when Walt Disney World opened in 1971. Always the forward thinker, Walt felt it was important to include Liberty Square in the new resort, further differentiating WDW from Disneyland.

Walt had plans to build an apartment on the upper floors of Cinderella Castle for himself and his family, much like the apartment in the Fire Station at Disneyland. Although the basic room was built, it was never completed as an apartment because Walt died before the park opened. Instead, WDW telephone operators worked there for many years, until 2007, when Imagineers renovated the space to create the Cinderella Castle Suite. The 650-square-foot suite was designed to include all modern amenities while exuding the feel of a true seventeenth-century chateau. As a touch of Disney magic, it even includes one special glass slipper on display. The suite is not for rent, though guests were randomly chosen to stay there during 2008's Year of a Million Dreams.

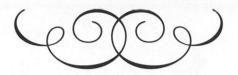

magineers who created the Morocco pavilion in Epcot are particularly proud of its authentic architecture, and they had some expert help to achieve it. King Hassan II took a great interest in Disney's spotlight on his country. To assess the pavilion's authenticity, he actually studied the Imagineers' scale model of the area prior to its construction. He even sent his personal architect to work with the Imagineering team on the project.

Disney found its four famous locomotives—the Walter E. Disney, the Lilly Belle, the Roy O. Disney, and the Roger E. Broggie—on the Yucatan Peninsula in Mexico. These trains, originally built by the Baldwin Locomotive Works of Philadelphia between 1916–28, were taken from the Yucatan and refurbished at the Tampa Shipbuilding and Dry Dock Company.

When Imagineers were designing Animal Kingdom, executives were unconvinced that the concept of an animal theme park would draw crowds and be able to compete with the many zoos around the country. To reassure them of the up-close and personal excitement of the safari attraction, Imagineers brought a live tiger into their presentation. That was all the convincing the top brass needed.

When you pass the lions on Kilimanjaro Safaris, don't be too afraid for yourself or the nearby animals that might normally serve as a tasty treat. Hidden from the visitors' view, an 18-foot-deep, 21-foot-wide moat separates the lions from other animals and the ride's vehicle path.

The famous catch phrase "I'm going to Disney World!" was first exclaimed by New York Giants MVP Phil Simms. It was his memorable response when asked, "What's next?" by a reporter directly after winning Super Bowl XXI in 1987. It triggered a series of very successful Disney commercials with sports celebrities such as L.A. Lakers' Magic Johnson, Dallas Cowboys' Emmitt Smith, New England Patriots' Tom Brady, and the Denver Broncos' John Elway.

ver wonder where all your recycled containers go? Well, quite a few milk jugs ended up in Animal Kingdom. Through Disney's efforts to be "green," the benches in the park are made of that recycled plastic material.

MILK

Ever heard of a "Weenie" at WDW? You've certainly seen them during your visits. This term is used for each of the park's "icons," or centerpieces. Walt felt they created a visual magnet, pulling visitors from one "land" to another. The idea first was executed at Disneyland in California and was so successful that it was carried over when WDW was built. Some hard-to-miss Weenies include Cinderella Castle, the Tree of Life, Spaceship Earth, and the giant Sorcerer Mickey hat.

Cast member roles are much more diverse than just attending the rides, dressing up in costumes, or working in hotels and restaurants. WDW actually has more than 3,000 different paid positions. Some of the more interesting jobs include topiary artists and designers, animal care aquarists (a.k.a. marine scientists), seamstresses, and even cosmetologists.

Love all those audio-animatronic figures in It's a Small World and elsewhere in the park? Approximately 1,100 audio-animatronic figures inhabit the Magic Kingdom alone, and about 2,000 populate the four theme parks in total. They're all controlled by one system, the Digital Animation Control System, otherwise known as DACS. This system coordinates about 72,000 individual audio-animatronic functions per second, along with 700 soundtracks. DACS is stationed in the utilidors under the Magic Kingdom.

Which original structure was the stave church, or "Stavkirke," in Epcot's Norway pavilion built to imitate? Gol Stave Church of Hallingdal, which was built in 1250 A.D., was the inspiration. Disney's version houses an exhibit on Norwegian culture, including the history of stave churches (medieval wooden churches with post-and-beam construction). At one point, more than 1,000 of these churches dotted Norway, where they were major components of the village center. Only

28 still stand today, and some of those are believed to be the oldest wooden structures in existence.

Can you name a WDW resident who is the proud parent of more than 500 offspring? More than 500 trees started out as mere acorns harvested by Disney horticulturists from the Liberty Tree in Liberty Square. This beautiful 130-year-old southern live oak stands in the center of Liberty Square in the Magic Kingdom. The 38-ton focal point is a tribute to Boston's original Liberty Tree and is believed to be one of the largest trees ever transplanted.

When you head out into Kilimanjaro Safaris in Animal Kingdom, you may think you just got lucky seeing so many animals up close. Is it chance? Nope! WDW encourages animals to spend time near the ride vehicles' sightlines by placing some food, a leafy plant called browse, close by. The browse is in feeders that are hard to notice since they're camouflaged as broken tree limbs and stumps. They look like a natural part of the landscape but are, in fact, made of concrete!

Ever notice the wooden leg labeled "Smith" among the props at the Frontierland Train Station? It's actually a nod to a silly joke you may remember in the floating tea party scene in the movie *Mary Poppins*. Bert comments, "Speaking of names, I know a man with a wooden leg named Smith." Uncle Albert asks, "What's the name of his other leg?"

Where can you find
one of the biggest animated props
in WDW? Splash Mountain's final scene
has a 36-foot-wide, 22-foot-high showboat
carrying 12 animated characters singing
"Zip-A-Dee-Doo-Dah" while the boat
rocks in time with the music.

You'll find about 3,000 fish swimming with many other fascinating sea creatures in the 5.7-million-gallon aquarium at The Seas with Nemo & Friends attraction in Epcot. The tank is 200 feet in diameter and 27 feet deep, making it one of the largest manmade ocean environments in the world. The artificial seawater required 27 truckloads of sodium chloride (common table salt).

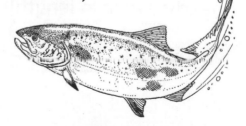

Opened three years later than scheduled, Test Track at Epcot claims fame for the most-delayed attraction in the history of the Disney parks. It also holds the title for the fastest ride (a top speed of 65mph) and longest ride (nearly a mile in length)!

The castle in Epcot's Japan pavilion is a replica of a seventeenth-century fortress, the Shirasagi-Jo (meaning "White Heron Castle"). The Shirasagi-Jo overlooks the city of Himeji and was designated a national treasure in 1931. In 1993 UNESCO added it to its World Cultural and Heritage Sites. It is considered one of the best-preserved castles in Japan.

Which park at WDW contains double the volume of rock work found at Mount Rushmore? Animal Kingdom showcases more than 1 million square feet of rock. That kind of volume could create a monolith 10 feet wide by 10 feet deep by two miles high!

Disney's housekeeping staff washes more than 285,000 pounds of laundry and dry-cleans at least 30,000 garments each and every day! That's the equivalent of you or I washing and drying two loads of laundry every day for 26 years!

WDW's opening day in 1971 went off fairly smoothly, although there was one arrest. A woman insisted she get free admission into the park because, she claimed, she was Cinderella. WDW's police cleverly convinced the confused lady to get in the police car by telling her it was a pumpkin.

Magic Kingdom's Toontown is getting its biggest makeover in history. Ground was broken on the expansion in 2010, and the project will be completed by 2013. Princesses—including Cinderella, Sleeping Beauty, Belle, and even Tinker Bell—will be the featured stars.

WDW has hosted weddings since 1991, helping couples from around the globe create their dream day in a way only Disney can. More than 40,000 weddings have been performed on the property. Disney's Wedding Pavilion opened in 1995, and several other ceremony locations are available as well. Brides and grooms can even get married before the sun comes up in the garden at Cinderella Castle.

Which WDW transformation required the use of nearly two dozen 40-foot candles, 1,000 feet of pink and blue (inflatable) "icing," 12 five-foot gumdrops, 30 three-foot lollipops, 16 five-foot candy bears, four six-foot Life Savers, 50 two-foot gum balls, several giant candy canes, 16 two-foot candy stars, and 400 gallons of pink paint? Cinderella Castle—when it was turned into an 18-story, pink-and-blue birthday cake for the resort's 15-month-long 25th Anniversary Celebration, which ran from 1996–98.

Oslo's fourteenth-century castle, Akershus, a national symbol in Norway and the seat for kings and government, is the primary inspiration for Norway's Akershus Royal Banquet Hall in Epcot. The restaurant seats 200 people for a smorgasbord-style dining experience. Disney princesses—Snow White, Belle, Aurora, Pocahontas, Ariel, and others—are even on hand during meal times.

WDW's Annual Epcot International Food and Wine Festival is one heck of a party. The event in 2010 served up 100,000 desserts, 33,000 bottles of wine and champagne, 3,000 gallons of soup, and 690,000 food samples—all doled out over 45 days.

The monorail system passes through the lobby of the Contemporary Resort, which opened alongside the Magic Kingdom and Polynesian Resort in 1971. Its modern, 14-story, A-frame, steel skeleton was constructed on site. Simultaneously, the individual rooms—including furnishings, plumbing, and electrical components—were built off-site three miles away. Later, each nine-ton prefabricated room was lifted into place by crane. Finally, a special sun-resistant glass was brought in to cover the entire structure.

The roof of Epcot's Universe of Energy is covered with two acres of solar panels that contain 80,000 photo-voltaic cells. The panels generate enough electricity to power the air-conditioning and the ride itself, hence the narrator's comment that you're "riding on sunshine." The Universe of Energy's solar-power system was the largest privately funded installation in the world when it opened in 1982.

Ever wonder why birds are scarce when you're walking around Epcot's Future World? After the park was built, staff members noticed birds building nests in inconvenient places and making themselves a bit of a nuisance. That's why Imagineers came up with a natural way to gently relocate these feathered residents. It's a birdcall repeating over and over that most visitors don't even notice. Imagineers installed a sound system with hidden speakers playing a "bird in distress" call to discourage other birds from making Future World their home.

Typhoon Lagoon's Crush 'n' Gusher is the only water roller coaster in North America that has three unique and separate rides you can experience from one tower. Each water nozzle propels guests along with 1,350 gallons of water per minute, creating enough water output off one slide to fill an average-size pool in just 60 seconds. The Crush n' Gusher can fill the 2.7-million-gallon Typhoon Lagoon wave pool in about three hours!

CINDERELLA CASTLE

10

spires were fabricated and finished five miles away from the resort in an old fertilizer factory

600

tons of steel were used to create the framework of the structure

189

feet high, the castle can be seen from two miles away, something that was important to Walt so visitors would be assured they were driving in the right direction after they got off the highway

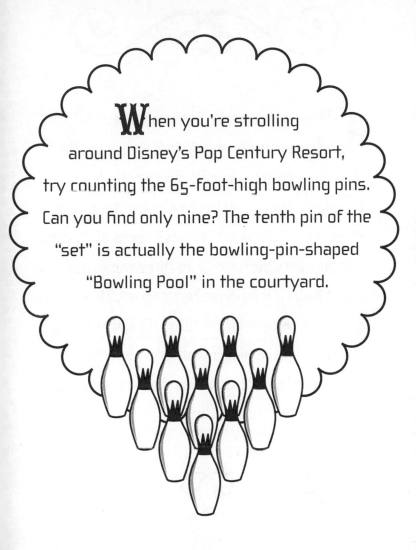

When you're strolling around Disney's Pop Century Resort, try counting the 65-foot-high bowling pins. Can you find only nine? The tenth pin of the "set" is actually the bowling-pin-shaped "Bowling Pool" in the courtyard.

WALT DISNEY WORLD
FACTS

Can you name a cast member job that requires nerves of steel? How about the precision drivers who perform the stunts at the Lights, Motors, Action! Extreme Stunt Show at Disney's Hollywood Studios? Teams of 20-plus cast members perform up to three shows per day of heart-stopping entertainment. These incredible drivers tackle 180s, 360s, fly-through-the-sky jumps, and many other tricks. The cars are actually outfitted with motorcycle engines for stunt-precision driving.

The WDW resort is the only resident in Lake Buena Vista, Florida. When Disney came in to develop the area, it persuaded government officials to create Lake Buena Vista, which is actually a Disney-governed municipality, providing the company with enormous control over the resort's development and operations.

Did you know that your pet can experience the magic of WDW, too? Best Friends Pet Care operates a facility across from Disney's Port Orleans Resort. The independently owned kennel offers 17,000 square feet of indoor space, 10,000 square feet of outdoor areas, and a 25,000-square-foot dog park. Travelers can leave their pets nearby in style while they visit the resort. You can even visit your dog and take him or her to a 1,300-square-foot "canines only" splash-and-play water area. Now that's a pampered pooch!

If you dare enter Animal Kingdom's Expedition Everest for a glimpse of its colossal audio-animatronic Yeti, you won't be disappointed. Disney went all out for an unforgettable encounter, creating one of the most advanced audio-animatronic characters ever. With all of the Yeti's hydraulic cylinders combined, it has a potential thrust of 259,000 pounds of force. This enables it to move very quickly and seem lifelike.

When you see cast members performing at WDW, remember, you may be catching a glimpse of a future star. Backstreet Boy Kevin Richardson is a former cast member who played Aladdin as well as one of the Teenage Mutant Ninja Turtles.

Ever wonder why Fire Station 71 in Town Square is numbered "71"? It's in honor of 1971, when the Magic Kingdom first opened.

The Living Character Initiative was developed by Imagineers using a combination of several technologies. The idea was to create characters that can interact and converse directly with the audience in a very life-like experience. They can even recognize and speak to specific guests. One such character is Crush the Turtle from Nemo & Friends' Turtle Talk with Crush. Disney first employed the Living Character Initiative when creating Lucky the Dinosaur, who can be seen in Animal Kingdom.

Who at WDW recited this pledge on October 10, 2010? "We pledge allegiance to the Society of 10-10-10 with fairness to all in the transaction of trading with the multitude of pins, we vow to honor the code of the fraternal order and perpetuate the activity of trading in our lives, our communities, and throughout the world for the betterment of all humankind." That would be the folks at the Disney Pin Trading Society 10-10-10 event at Disney's Yacht & Beach Club Convention Center. The free event launched the new decade of Disney pin trading, which has many enthusiastic members around the world.

The play area under the train trestle of Splash Mountain, called the Laughin' Place, was added to the attraction in 1997. It's intended to be a fun diversion for young visitors, who are not tall enough to ride, while they wait for family members.

WALT DISNEY WORLD
FACTS

In its 1994 redesign of Tomorrowland, the company refocused the park's original futuristic world—from what could be very real in the future to the new fantasy experience visitors get today. The new Tomorrowland is home to time travel, robots, spaceships battling aliens, Buzz Lightyear, the mischievous alien Stitch, and Monsters Inc.'s Mike Wazowski.

A 40-foot-tall Stratocaster guitar greets visitors at the entrance of the Rock 'n' Roller Coaster Starring Aerosmith in Hollywood Studios. The instrument's 32-foot-long neck morphs into a scale-model roller-coaster track, extending 320 feet to the entrance arch.

Why were plans for the Mount Fuji roller coaster ride scrapped in Epcot's Japan pavilion? Funding was an issue, along with Disney's relationship with Kodak, who was against indirect advertising for their competitor, the Fuji company.

Whether on the ground or in the air, Mickey Mouse is impressive. "Ear Force One," the giant Mickey Mouse-shaped hot air balloon that makes an occasional appearance over Walt Disney World, is more than 100 feet tall. The head of the balloon is 168 feet in diameter, and the ears are 35 feet in diameter. Uninflated and without the basket, Ear Force One weighs a whopping 330 pounds!

WDW has more than 34 different themed resorts, totaling nearly 28,000 hotel rooms—that's almost five times the number of accommodations in the MGM Grand in Las Vegas! WDW also features more than 3,000 Vacation Club units and 799 campsites.

Imagineers went to great pains to make Epcot's Das Kaufhaus similar to its inspiration, the Historisches Kaufhaus, a historic merchants hall in Freiburg, Germany. But which of the four original Habsburg emperors did the Disney building omit in order to keep it in proper scale with its surroundings? Philip I, Charles V, and Ferdinand I are all represented. Maximilian I, Holy Roman Emperor, was not represented.

Imagineers purchased more than 8,000 props, mostly from Nepal, to augment authenticity at the village of Expedition Everest. The artifacts include yeti dolls, antique Chinese ceramics, waterproof barrels designed for mountain journeys, and a Mani Rimdu dance costume typically worn by a monk during a two-week festival.

Instead of your standard "zoo" experience with animals in cages and on constant display, Animal Kingdom's Kilimanjaro Safaris' Imagineers created a much more natural environment in which the animals live and roam freely. This allows the animals to play a little peek-a-boo with visitors, adding to the excitement and realism of the "safari" experience.

isney had to shell out an incredible $400 million to build WDW by opening day on October 1, 1971. Compare that with the national average wage at the time— $6,497, and the average price of a new home—only $24,300.

What was the previous name of the *Liberty Belle* riverboat that plies the Rivers of America in the Magic Kingdom? *Richard F. Irvine* was the boat's original name until 1996, when it was renamed *Liberty Belle*. Mr. Irvine was the former vice president and director of design for the Walter Elias Disney Company, later called WDI. Disney felt the new name would better represent the boat's ties to Liberty Square.

The seemingly old, cracked, sun-blanched asphalt guests walk on near Primeval Whirl in the Animal Kingdom isn't asphalt at all. It's concrete extensively treated to look like it. When Disneyland opened its doors in California, Imagineers realized the asphalt they laid down was a poor choice. The heat-softened surface allowed pointed objects like high heels to sink in and sometimes get stuck. Disney didn't make the same mistake twice.

If you've been inside Mexico's Plaza de los Amigos in Epcot more than once, you might have noticed that the lighting is always set to portray twilight. In Mexican culture, twilight is the time friends and family gather in the plaza to socialize.

Where can you find 56 high-definition cameras (42 of which are robotic), 40 high-definition video screens, and a 20-zone audio system? The ESPN Wide World of Sports Complex at WDW, which also includes the ESPN Innovation Lab, where groundbreaking, on-air products such as 3-D telecast technology are being developed.

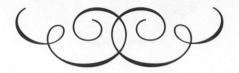

When Disney developed the land for the resort, it installed approximately 55 miles of canals and levees to control water levels without depleting the overall reserve. But instead of employing the usual straight path canal design, which is more invasive, Imagineer John Hench came up with a more attractive idea: a canal system that curves along with the existing landscape.

Which WDW thrill ride clocks speeds faster than Space Mountain? Frontierland's Splash Mountain, built in 1992, drops you 52-feet at a 45-degree angle, creating a breathtaking 40mph adventure.

Ever want your own little piece of Disney property? Some folks actually purchase homes in Walt Disney World's resort. The Golden Oak residential resort community, now in development, offered fewer than 30 home sites for sale beginning in 2010, ranging from $1.5 million to $8 million each. Homeowners work with Disney-approved builders to choose between different Disney-approved styles of construction. The gated community will feature many special amenities, including a full-service spa, golf course, VIP transportation into the parks, tickets to special park events, and many other perks.

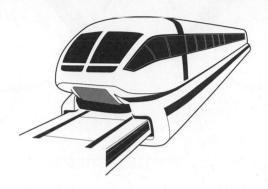

The monorail, WDW's most famous mode of travel, wasn't actually invented by Disney. It was patented by Henry Palmer of Great Britain in 1821. Imagineers put their own futuristic modifications on it, though, thus creating its high-tech look. When Disney constructed WDW, Imagineers increased the width and length of the original Disneyland-style monorail cars in order to provide the sleek transportation system necessary for the giant park.

When you glimpse the tigers in the Maharajah Jungle Trek, in the Asia section of Animal Kingdom, you may see them sleeping. Tigers spend 18 to 20 hours a day catching zzz's. Disney uses a program called "Enrichment" to encourage the tigers to wake during park hours. This includes randomly adding novel things to the animals' environment, which may stimulate them and encourage natural behaviors.

A Sleeping Beauty ride originally was included in the concept stages of the Magic Kingdom, but it was replaced by Snow White's Scary Adventures. Aurora will have her chance to shine in the Magic Kingdom's renovations, which are slated to be revealed in 2013. Other rides that were planned but never made it to construction included an Ichabod Crane Headless Horseman ride and a Jolly Holiday with Mary Poppins attraction.

Think you have a lot of holiday decorations to unpack and set up each year? WDW hauls out more than 1,500 Christmas trees, 11 miles of garlands, 3,000 wreaths, 300,000 yards of ribbon, and 8 million lights to decorate the park for each holiday season. Now that's festive!

At WDW's Toy Story Mania!, guests get to experience what life is like from a toy's perspective by coming into contact with View-Master reels nearly four feet in diameter and Tinkertoy connectors that are two feet across. Andy's Room will make a 5'6" person feel about 14 inches tall.

Over a three-year period, Animal Kingdom came to life on what was a barren cow pasture. The incredible transformation included laying 60 miles of plumbing, importing 4.4 million yards of dirt, creating rivers, and relocating animals from around the world—all for a reported investment of $800 million!

The 16-million-pound Spaceship Earth, the centerpiece of Epcot, is 165 feet in diameter, enclosing 2.2 million cubic feet of space inside. It's actually constructed of two spheres. The inner layer is sealed in a thick rubber coating, while the outer layer is covered in 11,324 unbreakable, weather-resistant, aluminum and plastic alloy triangles called "alucobond"—each piece is a custom fit. Rainwater never falls off this famous sphere, because it's channeled inside the ball and caught by a gutter system, funneling it away and into the lagoon.

Did you know that WDW came very close to being built in St. Louis, Missouri? While in St. Louis, finalizing plans, Walt had a last-minute change of heart after being insulted by one of the city's most influential business leaders. August (Gussie) Busch Jr. remarked: "Any man who thinks he can design an attraction that is going to be a success in this city and not serve beer or liquor ought to have his head examined." This prompted Walt to board his plane the following morning and scrap all plans for that location. Walt felt strongly that selling alcohol was not in line with the Disney image and was offended when his business sense was questioned. Although the city tried to change his mind, Walt turned his attention to Florida instead.

**WALT DISNEY WORLD
FACTS**

What building at China's showcase in Epcot is meant to symbolize the Chinese universe? The Temple of Heaven—which is half the size of its inspiration, the Summer Palace in Bejing—has many intricate details inside, each symbolic in Chinese culture.

The animals in Animal Kingdom's Africa don't spend the night outside as they would in the wild. They are actually "tucked in" every night in Disney's Night Houses, each specifically designed by experts to suit the species it hosts. The amazing thing is how they get there: Each species has been trained by Disney professionals to respond to a unique audio cue. When they hear their cue—a beating drum, bell, etc.—they head to their sleeping quarters. While they snooze, Disney's gardeners head out early in the morning to plant and prune the area to keep up with the animals' feeding habits.

Did you know that in each of the Toy Story Mania! attraction games, there's a hidden "Easter egg"? (In computer-speak, "Easter eggs" are hidden messages or objects.) If you happen to find one, it will trigger other bonus high-value targets and even changes in the scene. Happy hunting!

Over the course of each year, 4,000 hanging baskets are grown and distributed throughout WDW. The planning process begins a year in advance, with an eye toward matching seasonal flowering trees and surrounding architecture. About 800 of these baskets are displayed on any given day.

Although the *Admiral Joe Fowler* riverboat was one of the originally planned attractions at WDW, it was not part of the resort's opening day on October 1, 1971. It actually opened just one day later, on October 2. Peter Pan's Flight opened the day after that, on October 3.

The initial installation of WDW's 14-mile monorail system reportedly cost $14 million, a sizable amount of money in 1971. The trains are now made with a fiberglass composite over steel-frame bodies. Disney is so dedicated to their maintenance that the monorail system runs at 99.9 percent efficiency almost all year long. That's a happy statistic for the approximately 50 million people per year who ride it!

What massive park icon or "Weenie" required an actual oil rig to support part of its design? The Tree of Life has thousands of colossal, artificial branches and more than 100,000 leaves, making it so heavy that Disney had to incorporate a giant oil rig inside the structure to support the massive weight of the limbs.

The beautiful, intricate mosaic murals on the archway walls of Cinderella Castle were designed by Disney artist Dorothea Redmond. It took two years for craftsman Hanns-Joachim Scharff and his team to render them. The story, which tells Cinderella's journey, is constructed of approximately 1 million pieces of multicolor Italian glass, silver, and 14-karat gold.

The inspiration for the idealistic Main Street U.S.A. was Marceline, Missouri—Walt's hometown. The family moved there in 1906 when the Disneys bought a nearby 45-acre farm. They left in 1910 for Kansas City, Missouri. Walt had fond memories of the little 5,000-resident town.

The photos hanging in the Expedition Everest Himalayan Village "museum" were taken by Joe Rohde, executive designer at Walt Disney Imagineering and lead designer of Animal Kingdom, while on his research trip to Nepal for the attraction's village, Serka Zong.

The first phase of Epcot took exactly three years (October 1, 1979–October 1, 1982) to build, requiring almost 3,000 designers and 4,000 construction workers, whose duties included excavating 54 million cubic feet of dirt. Epcot's total area covers 305 acres, more than twice the size of the Magic Kingdom.

Weird things always seem to turn up in the lost-and-found bin at WDW. Some of the more bizarre items include a prosthetic leg, a glass eye, and a potty training seat. The owners eventually claimed each of those items. On the tamer side, sunglasses are commonly turned in, too—more than 35,000 pair a year!

Disney's Eiffel Tower in Epcot's France showcase was built to a one-tenth scale but still maintains the feel of the original size. That's quite a trick. Some of the ways Disney accomplishes this are by using forced perspective, setting the tower far back so it needs to be viewed from a distance, and even installing bird deterrents. "Giant" birds perched on the Eiffel Tower would certainly detract from the illusion of its size!

What cars have a whopping 22 wheels and six braking systems? Epcot's Test Track vehicles. Although these cars only show four wheels to visitors, they're riding on a lot more. The three onboard computers pack more combined processing power than NASA's Space Shuttle.

Why is Exposition Hall on Main Street U.S.A. the only building built to full scale? The other buildings on the street employ scale changes on the upper floors to increase their height perception. Exposition Hall was the exception, because Imagineers wanted to block the view of the Contemporary Resort behind it.

What part of Animal Kingdom originally was going to be named Genesis Gardens? The Oasis, at the front of the park. Disney felt "Genesis Gardens" had too strong a religious connotation, and decided Oasis was less controversial and more true to the area's intended purpose.

Enormous pine logs harvested from standing dead wood at an elevation of 7,000 feet in Oregon and Montana were used in the construction of Disney's Wilderness Lodge. Imagineers used National Park lodges like the Old Faithful Inn at Yellowstone and the Ahwahnee Lodge in Yosemite for their inspiration.

How many people attended WDW on September 15, 1999, in spite of Hurricane Floyd's presence off the coast? None. As a safety precaution, WDW completely closed the parks for the first time in history. In fact, they closed the parks early on Tuesday, September 14, as well. That day, Floyd's hurricane-force winds extended 125 miles from the storm's eye, and sustained winds up to 140mph triggered massive evacuations in southeastern states.

The height of guests' sightline in the safari truck of Kilimanjaro Safaris was carefully taken into account by Imagineers, who determine what they want you to see and what they don't want you to see. There are also many hidden barriers that allow the animals to seemingly roam free and mix together as they would in nature, but in fact they don't. This is clearly for safety reasons. The animals are kept separate through camouflaged fences, impassable bridges, and even a barrier in the water to prevent hippos from getting too close to the ride vehicles when they pass through the river.

Who is one of WDW's favorite cast members for pin-trading enthusiasts? That would be Scoop Anderson, *Main Street Gazette* reporter, town councilman, and avid pin trader. This "pin-thusiast" became so popular with folks that Disney made a series of pins featuring or inspired by Scoop.

WDW has created some handy pit stops for moms and dads with babies. Did you know each of WDW's four theme parks has a Baby Care Center? They feature diaper changing rooms; feeding rooms equipped with highchairs, bibs, and plastic spoons; private rooms with rocking chairs for nursing; and even formula and diapers for sale.

The Main Street U.S.A. window honoring Frank Wells, former Disney president and CEO, includes the imaginary company name "Seven Summits Expeditions," giving us a hint to his love for mountain climbing. In the Disney tradition for detail, they further emphasized it by placing his sign in the highest window on Main Street.

Ever notice the pavement stamp "Mortimer Bros. Construction Co. 1928" on the sidewalk by the L.A. Prop Shop in the Hollywood Studios park? The year is a nod to the release date of Mickey Mouse's first film, *Steamboat Willie*. But why Mortimer Bros? Before finally settling on "Mickey," "Mortimer" was the first name Walt bestowed upon his beloved mouse.

Why are the elevator motors in the Tower of Terror actually sealed inside the building? Because they're so massive, at 12-feet tall and 35-feet long, that they weigh a whopping 132,000 pounds, generating enough torque to equal 275 Corvette engines. They had to be lifted by crane into place, and the building was then completed around them, sealing them in.

WOW is dedicated to diversity, even when it comes to horticulture. You can find more than 3,000 plant species throughout the resort, including plants from the 50 states and 50 countries. The only continent not represented is Antarctica.

Want some helpful advice on planning your family's trip to WDW? Because most people today head to the Internet for information, Walt Disney World created DisneyWorldMoms.com in 2008. The site features a question-and-answer venue with Disney-approved moms and dads from around the country who have the scoop on planning a great trip to the resort. The 2010 panel consists of 21 new Disney World "experts," as well as 22 returning panelists.

What's unique about the window reading "Walt Disney World Railroad Office, keeping dreams on track, Walter E. Disney, Chief Engineer," on the front of the Train Station on Main Street U.S.A.? It's the only window that can be seen from outside the park.

The first building on Main Street U.S.A. is the WDW Railroad office. The sign in the window states "Walt Disney World Railroad Office, keeping dreams on track, Walter E. Disney, Chief Engineer." It's interesting to note that Walt is also honored in the last window on Main Street. Above the Plaza Restaurant you'll see, "Walt Disney, Master Classes in Design and Master Planning." Think of this like movie credits, where the producer gets the first and last nod.

It's intentional that you can't see the bottom of the 1.9-million-gallon moat used for Hollywood Studios' Fantasmic! show. The water is only 1½-feet deep, so Disney leaves some algae in it, even though it's filtered and treated, in order to mask its depth.

Ever wonder why the Roman numeral clock on front of Cinderella Castle has a "IIII" representing 4, instead of "IV"? The "IIII" and "IV" were interchangeable in ancient Roman times, and "IIII" makes it easier for people to differentiate between 4 and 6.

Disney's horticultural efforts began before the resort even opened in 1971, with the creation of a tree farm. More than 8,000 trees were present in their initial inventory, along with another 1,500 trees in transit, which had been moved from areas Disney was developing. Plants from around the world, including Asia, Africa, and Australia, also were brought there and adapted to Florida's climate and soil. Some of those plants took more than three years to acclimate.

The second-floor
shop window on Main Street U.S.A.,
reading "Dolls by Miss Joyce, Dollmaker
for the World," is in honor of Disney legend
Joyce Carlson, who had built dolls and
their costumes for every It's a Small
World attraction, including the 1964–65
World's Fair in New York.

Eight hundred concrete piles, extending a whopping 70 feet down into the ground, provide the foundation for WDW's Bay Lake Towers at the Contemporary Resort. If these were stacked one on top of another, they would climb more than 10 miles into the sky.

If the Test Track experience leaves you wanting even more speed, or you've always dreamed about being a race-car driver, sign up for the Richard Petty Driving Experience. For a wide range of prices, you can drive authentic Winston Cup-style stock cars capable of up to 145mph on a one-mile tri-oval track—after some instruction, of course. You'll need some cash for the dash. The most elaborate package costs more than $1,000.

Ever wonder where Disney got the 4½ miles of white sand for the beaches around Seven Seas Lagoon and Bay Lake? It wasn't there when Disney bought the property, but it was close by. After Disney drained Bay Lake during the first stages of the resort's construction, workers dredged out muck and debris from the bottom. Underneath, they found thousands of tons of white sand, which they cleaned and later placed around the perimeter once Seven Seas Lagoon was built.

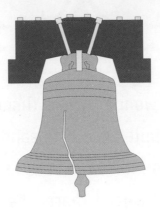

iberty Square's Liberty Bell was actually cast from the very same mold used to create the original, famous bell in Philadelphia. Disney placed the bell in Liberty Square in 1987 to commemorate the U.S. Constitution's bicentennial.

Walt made one thing certain when he chose a location for WDW. He wanted a large amount of land in order to pursue every avenue the company came up with to entertain its guests, and he insisted on better control of the resort's surrounding area, as well. This was Walt's frustration with Disneyland. He got his wish in Florida. In fact, Disneyland could fit into WDW 100 times over.

The original plans for the Kali River Rapids in the Asia section of Animal Kingdom contained three small drops. But once it was mocked up, Imagineers felt it didn't have enough impact. So, instead, the drops were combined into what is now the single, 25-foot drop that plunges riders down into the water, ensuring a good soaking for everyone aboard.

Can you name the first attraction in which Disney offered two variations of the same ride? Mission Space at Epcot. Although many people love this attraction for its thrill factor, others felt it could be toned down a bit. Disney decided to offer two versions in order to broaden the appeal of Mission Space. Choose the Orange Team for the intense experience mimicking what an astronaut might go through, or the Green Team, for a less intense galactic adventure.

If you ever thought you could build a better ride than Expedition Everest, Space Mountain, or the Rock 'n' Roller Coaster, you can try at Disney Quest in the Downtown Disney West Side waterfront entertainment complex. In this indoor, interactive theme park consisting of five floors with more than 250 arcade games and eight different attractions, you'll find the popular CyberSpace Mountain. This feature lets you build your own roller-coaster ride with barrel rolls, flips, and multiple inversions. Then you get the thrill of experiencing your custom-designed ride in a 360-degree motion simulator.

id you ever wonder why the Emporium on Main Street U.S.A. has a sign above one of the doorways claiming it was established in 1901? That's the year Walt Disney was born. Main Street U.S.A. is an especially good place to look for little details like this that Imagineers tucked around Walt Disney World.

ABOUT THE AUTHOR

Laurie Flannery is a writer, sound recording engineer, and mom to three small explorers. She's written for several magazines, and has more than 15 years of experience in the recording studio. When she's not off on an adventure with her kids, she prefers to spend her time creating, writing, and delving into the arts, sciences, and all things related to parenting. She resides in New England.